CONTENTS

Foreword iii

Summary v

1 The context 1
Impetus for the study 1
Historical background 3
The role of the arts funding system in the 1990s 3

2 The current landscape 9
The 1998/99 portfolio 10

3 Situational analysis 27
The art 27
Economics 30
Access 34

4 Mapping the future 35
Important trends 35
Interactive consumption 36
Implications for dance 37

5 Priorities for investing in 21st century dance 41
Investing in individuals 41
Strengthening companies 43
Facing the future 44
Creating the climate 45
The results 46

Appendixes
1 A short history of dance 49
2 Growth in Arts Council funds for dance 1969/70 to 1998/99 51
3 Regularly funded dance organisations in England 1998/99 52
4 Touring dance companies 54
5 Sources 56

Index 57

Foreword

The story of dance in England over the last few decades is a testament to the impact and benefits of the strategic investment of public funding in the arts. This investment has released the creative energies of dance artists, enabled diversity and innovation in dance languages and meanings, and has brought many ways of engaging with dance to people of all ages across the country. Our understanding of dance today includes world class dancers and choreographers, dance works that challenge and entertain, and pioneering opportunities for participation in dance.

These are achievements to celebrate. They have been hard won. However, there is more to be done. Public investment has nurtured growth but has lacked the capacity to keep pace with the creative energy of dance artists. This has brought disappointment and frustration. So, while being proud of our history, we must learn from experience and look forwards. This is the aim of *21st century dance*.

This book is the result of a lengthy and considered process. Commissioned by the Arts Council of England's Dance Advisory Panel, it has benefited from the contribution of Panel members at every stage. It briefly documents the recent history of dance into the new millennium, provides a situational analysis, looks forward to urging those who work in, enjoy or support dance to anticipate the future and concludes with a vision for investing in the future-readiness of dance.

21st century dance demonstrates that dance has achieved much – but too quietly; and that it has built notable strengths in innovation, diversity and education – but too often at the cost of reasonable salaries, working conditions and career progression for its practitioners. The opportunity to create a step-change must be seized.

It is time to face the future. The opportunity to leap confidently forward is here. It requires sustained investment, courage and ambition. In return, dance can guarantee creative diversity, challenge, innovation and the potential to provide socially relevant, dynamic and inspiring experiences for the artists and audiences of the 21st century.

Professor Christopher Bannerman
Chair, Arts Council of England Dance Advisory Panel

Please note: In March 2001, just before this publication went to print, the Arts Council announced a £3.2 million increase over two years for the dance companies and organisations within its portfolio. This book provides an overview of dance in England into the new millennium, leading up to that announcement.

Summary

Dance portfolio

Dance in England has found new languages, forms, meanings and applications over the last four decades. In 1969/70, the Arts Council supported seven dance organisations; in 1998/99 this number grew to 74 and encompassed a far wider range of artistic visions, purposes and ways of working. Today the funded dance portfolio is diverse and eclectic, including performing companies, dance agencies providing promotion and space for creation, production and participation, and strategic development organisations. Access, education and new ways of engaging with audiences have been integral to this growth.

The Arts Council established its Dance department in 1979. In 1989, Graham Devlin's *Stepping Forward* provided a blueprint for the following decade with a focus on developing a healthy dance ecology. Achievements during the 1990s included the establishment of National Dance Agencies, the growth of a number of new companies and significant growth in audiences. Dance has been nurtured to the point of maturity, but its critical mass is still developing. While it provides work and audiences for a range of other art forms, with relatively few sustainable commercial outlets the dance economy remains particularly reliant on the arts funding system. Maturing at what was a time of shrinkage in real terms in public funding for the arts, it is perhaps inevitable that creative energy has outstripped public investment.

Analysis of the 54 dance organisations receiving regular funding from the regional arts boards and the Arts Council in 1998/99 shows that the majority (24) were agencies, followed closely by companies (22). Almost 80% of all organisations received grants of less than £250k, while almost 50% of the funds went to only 4% of the longest established organisations. London is the main production centre and is home to most of the largest organisations, although there is a more equitable geographical distribution of dance agencies. While ballet received about three-quarters of the funds, it also provides almost half of all performances, two-thirds of jobs for dancers, almost three-quarters of all audiences, and good value for money when compared to its peer group of arts organisations.

Almost all dance companies tour. There are no dance companies with their own theatres. The Royal Ballet performs mainly at the Royal Opera House, which it shares with the Royal Opera, and Birmingham Royal Ballet is based in the Birmingham Hippodrome Theatre, which it shares with a range of art forms. Dance still needs to develop a countrywide network of appropriate venues. Demand for large-scale dance remains strong, but on the smaller scales dates tend to be spasmodic and runs restricted to one or two performances. There is a wide range of choice for promoters, and a regular diet of international work is touring more widely. But under-resourced theatres demand significant marketing and audience development support from even more stretched dance companies. This is particularly onerous on the smaller scales where management resources are leanest and budgets tightest. A number of these dance companies have been facing crises. Beyond the traditional theatre context, dance is having a powerful impact in site-specific work, and digital dance. There is potential for further diversification in the means of disseminating dance to new and wider audiences.

Structural investment *Jonzi D*

Individual artists are driving the art form forwards. The introduction of Dance Fellowships in 2000/01 recognises this and has been widely welcomed by the sector. Dancers also need creative opportunities, and the creative energies of dance managers, teachers, commentators and facilitators need to be fostered for the benefit of dance's future. Essentially collaborative, dance is looking to its own resources and building partnerships across and beyond the sector in order to tackle issues collectively.

Dancers' performing careers are short and precarious. Most dancers work on short contracts, and stop performing in their 30s. Many embark on their careers with debt accumulated over three or four years of full-time training, and they need to sustain a maintenance programme of regular class and complementary techniques. Injury is a constant risk, and while improvements have been made in understanding its prevention and management such measures have a cost implication. There is a need to recognise these factors. Improved salaries while dancing, and opportunities for professional development that equip dancers for post-performing careers in dance, would help stem the flow of experience and expertise out of the sector.

Salaries, salary progression, working conditions and continuous professional development are major issues across dance. For an industry that is entirely dependent on people, the lack of regular, structural investment in its people is remarkable, and encouraged by reliance on public funding.

Future-ready

Life is changing, and unless we look to the future, we are in danger of proposing solutions for yesterday's problems. There are opportunities for dance in providing real and virtual interactive art experiences, high-impact special events, and in its transient, experimental, collaborative and essentially human qualities. At the same time, digitalisation offers the potential for the commodification of dance, with the associated possibility of reducing its reliance on public funding. Yet the possibility of piracy and need for commercial acumen could inhibit benefit. Increasingly the future will require those working in dance to take risks, yet the traditional model of public funding for the arts provides neither the potential for gain nor a baseline of security. Dance celebrates and is enriched by cultural diversity, yet a decade of decline in funding for vocational training has resulted in a student population that is predominantly white, middle-class and female. Much of the traditional culture of training and working practice encourages conformity rather than difference. Individuals will drive the major changes in dance, and the arts funding system's recent focus on individuals offers an opportunity to support individual vision, talent and drive. It is time to build in the capacity for dance to be future-ready, if not future-proof.

The vision for *21st century dance* weaves together strengthened core support with shifts in approach – focused on individuals and companies, looking to the future and creating the climate in which dance can thrive. Backing for individuals could build on the Arts Council Dance Fellowships Programme to include dancers, others working in dance and promoters and producers. Companies at all scales need to be strengthened, with backing directed at anticipating growth and releasing capacity. Seismic shifts could be initiated by creative coalitions between organisations, while the potential to back the unexpected needs to be built in. A climate conducive to dance would provide special attention for cultural diversity, build the capacity of strategic organisations, release the capacity of dance agencies and nurture regional dance ecologies. Running through this vision are the core values of quality, diversity, inclusivity, access and education.

1 The context

IMPETUS FOR THE STUDY

The arts funding system has played a significant role in the growth and development of dance over the latter part of the 20th century. This study focuses on those parts of dance that have directly benefited from public subsidy, but does so with a keen awareness of the wealth and diversity of other dance contexts.

The impetus for this study was a strengthening awareness by the Arts Council's Dance Advisory Panel that, a decade after *Stepping Forward*[1] had provided a blueprint for dance in the 1990s, it was time to take stock and look to a new future.

The drivers for change at the start of the 21st century included:

- new structures and values across the arts funding system
- new strategic priorities and changing role for the Arts Council of England
- new funds and sources of funds
- a government agenda that recognises the importance of culture
- a dynamic climate conducive to change
- the growing maturity of the dance sector
- evident strains and signs of fragility across the dance sector

[1] Devlin, *Stepping Forward* 1989

HISTORICAL BACKGROUND

The recent history of dance is short and art-led[2]. At the end of WWII, the Arts Council supported two classical ballet companies (Sadler's Wells Theatre Ballet and Ballet Rambert), and the modern Ballets Jooss. The 1950s saw the establishment of London Festival Ballet (now English National Ballet), and Western Theatre Ballet (which became Scottish Ballet in 1969). The 1960s witnessed the reinvention of Ballet Rambert from a classical to a modern ensemble company, the establishment of the school and performing company at The Place and the beginnings of new dance experiments. In the 1970s Northern Ballet Theatre was established in Manchester, accompanied by further growth and diversification and, in 1979, the establishment of the Arts Council's Dance Department. The 1980s saw growth in animateurs and companies, the first Dance Umbrella Festival, the birth of Dance UK and the Foundation for Community Dance, and the establishment of degrees in dance. Access, education and finding new ways of engaging with audiences have been integral to artistic developments. Examples include the residencies undertaken by London Contemporary Dance Theatre in the 1970s, X6's publication of its *New Dance* journal and the growth of community dance.

LEFT:
Rambert Dance Company / Rooster

THE ROLE OF THE ARTS FUNDING SYSTEM IN THE 1990s

Dance agencies

Over the last decade, the strategies of the arts funding system, coupled with the artistic creativity and entrepreneurial approach of the dance constituency, have resulted in significant changes in the dance landscape. A modest increase in the Arts Council's allocation to dance in the early 1990s established the first National Dance Agencies (NDAs), to facilitate the growth of

[2] See appendix 1, A short history of dance; appendix 2, Growth in Arts Council funds for dance 1969/70 to 1998/99

communities of dance artists and focal points for dance across England. NDAs provide strategically managed meeting points for dance creation, production, participation and promotion. Increasingly they are driving the art form forward: commissioning new work, specialising in future-facing issues such as dance on screen and the nurturing of artistic development, and establishing their national and international significance. The concept and model built on community dance experience has cascaded to local level, enabling NDAs to increasingly develop their strategic roles.

National, regional and county dance agencies accounted for 24 of the 54 dance organisations receiving regular funding from the Arts Council and the regional arts boards (RABs) in 1998/99, and for most of those regularly funded by RABs[3]. Some attract local authority support. In 1998/99[4] this ranged from £1,130 for Dance Agency Cornwall, to £96,947 for Ludus Dance Agency. This vital part of the infrastructure is less than 10 years old but is already proving invaluable in supporting artists and bringing people and dance together. It could be seen as the dance equivalent of the national network of producing theatres yet between them, these 24 key organisations received a total of only £2 million from the arts funding system in 1998/99.

Dance companies

Some RABs have provided sustained funding to companies and other dance organisations, for example to Jabadao, Ludus and Phoenix Dance Company. This has enabled their continued growth and increased the diversity of the subsidised portfolio. At the Arts Council, Adzido and Dance Umbrella have moved from annual to regular funding. Extemporary Dance Company, ADiTi, and the Black Dance Development Trust have closed. The Kosh, Second Stride, Michael Clark and Nahid Siddiqui

3 See appendix 3, and Scope and scale of grants, p 10

4 Taken from the information submitted for the survey of performance indicators

have now moved from regular funding to a range of methods of funding support. The proportion of budget allocated to the national companies, Royal Ballet and Birmingham Royal Ballet, has decreased from 53% to 51%[5]. In 2000/01 Dance Fellowships for individual artists were introduced.

5 See appendix 2

The major growth area, and the one that best signifies the maturing of the dance sector, is that of fixed-term funding. Companies and organisations that were emerging, artistically and managerially, at the start of the 1990s now have established artistic track records, organisational structures and national strategic roles. Arts Council expenditure on this area has increased from £900k in 1990/91 to almost £3 million in 1998/99, but this sum still only accounts for 13% of the total Arts Council dance budget. Green Candle and Shobana Jeyasingh were funded through this category in 1990/91. By the end of the decade, it included Badejo Arts, CandoCo, Cholmondeleys and Featherstonehaughs, DV8, Siobhan Davies, Union Dance, V-Tol, and Yolande Snaith. Adventures in Motion Pictures grew through project to fixed-term funding and is now a thriving commercial organisation.

Shobana Jeyasingh Dance Company / Intimacies of the Third Order

Development organisations

The prime purpose of the Arts Council's dance

strategy over the last decade has been to create a healthy ecology for dance. Dance UK and the Foundation for Community Dance both began as artist-led initiatives and have emerged as strategic development organisations dealing respectively with the wellbeing of dance, dancers, choreographers and managers, and the application of dance in wider social contexts. Their work complements that of NDAs and generic professional organisations such as Equity and the Independent Theatre Council. Culturally-specific development organisations such as The Black Dance Development Trust and ADiTi have had a more mixed history, and now the South Asian Dance Consortium is gaining in strength while the Association of Dance of the African Diaspora is reviewing its role and remit. English dance has an enviable reputation internationally for its cultural diversity, quality, creativity and the relative strength of its infrastructure. These are the rewards of three decades of investment of time and money, of evolving strategies and a dynamic partnership between artists and the arts funding system.

Overview

In recent years, the relationship between artists and the arts funding system has often been characterised by frustration with the funding system's inability to respond quickly and adequately to the creative energy of artists[6]. The reasons for this are partly historic, resulting from dance's relatively late arrival at the funding table[7]. Appendix 2 demonstrates the growth in Arts Council spending on dance. Excluding the national companies, spending between 1969/70 and 1998/99 grew significantly. Over the same period, the number of organisations supported grew ten-fold, from seven to 74. This has resulted in a decline in the average spending per organisation, from £26.8k in 1969/70 to £16.4k in 1998/99.

[6] *Independent dance sector review report*, Gill Clarke and Rachel Gibson; June 1998

[7] See appendix 1, *A short history of dance*

Dance's growth at what was a time of declining government funding for the arts[8], and of competing claims from established organisations experiencing financial crisis, has exacerbated the gulf between opportunity and investment. Being essentially people rather than building based, and with a national rather than specifically local or regional profile, most dance companies have not attracted significant funds from local authorities. Nor has dance been in a position to compete for sponsorship against the more established performing arts such as opera and drama. Consequently, dance is currently particularly reliant on the arts funding system.

8 See appendix 2. The Arts Council's grant in aid to the arts declined from around £23.5m in 1989/90 to around £20.3m in 1998/99 (compared in the equivalent of 1969/70 prices)

2
The current landscape

Dance is one of the oldest art forms and yet it has been significantly reinventing its languages, forms, meanings and applications over the last four decades. This process of renewal can be seen in the changes of range and type of work that the arts funding system has supported over this period. In the latter part of the 20th century, dance experienced the kind of artistic revolution that transformed the visual arts post-impressionism. As a result, we now enjoy possibly the richest, widest ranging and most dynamic dance diet of any time since the tag 'the dancing English' was coined some 500 years ago[9].

Dance has established value in education, health, social cohesion and regeneration. Research undertaken by the Foundation for Community Dance identified over 73,000 participatory projects, and found that community dance projects engaged over 4.7 million people in 2000[10]. Dancers and choreographers earn a living in classical, contemporary and culturally diverse dance forms, in theatre, opera, film, musicals, music videos/DVDs, television advertisements and internationally. Audiences and participants have more choice than ever between where and how they engage with dance, and between cultural and artistic voices.

Audiences for dance are growing. The recession in the early 1990s saw a decline in audiences for all performing

[9] *Ballet, an illustrated history*: Mary Clarke and Clement Crisp; Adam and Charles Black; London; 1974 (page 28)

[10] Foundation for Community Dance – National Mapping Research project, 2000

arts, but audiences for dance have grown by 13.7%[11] over the last six years and increased by 18% between 1997/98 and 1998/99[12]. The picture for contemporary dance is even healthier. Comparing Target Group Index (TGI) average results for the five-year period of 1990/91 to 1994/95 with those for the period 1995/96 to 1999/2000 shows an increase in audiences for contemporary dance of 28.8%.

THE 1998/99 PORTFOLIO

Analysing the 1998/99[13] portfolio of dance organisations regularly funded by the RABs and the Arts Council provides a snapshot of subsidised dance provision in terms of regional spread, type of organisation, dance form and touring provision.

This snapshot examines core funded dance activity. Over the same period a further £700k, distributed through venue and promoter initiatives, supported dance touring.

Scope and scale of grants

Fifty-four organisations are included in the survey: 24 agencies, 22 companies, seven other organisations and Ludus, which is both a company and an agency. A full list is given in appendix 3, which also identifies their location, main funding body and level of regular funding.

The total funding to these 54 organisations was just over £24 million. Thirty-seven per cent of organisations received grants of less than £50k. Graph 1 (right) demonstrates the spread of grants and shows that while 80% of organisations received 14% of the funds, 4% of organisations received almost 50% of the funds.

---

[11] *Roles and Functions of the English Regional Producing Theatres*; Peter Boyden Associates for the Arts Council of England; May 2000

[12] *Statistical survey of regularly funded organisations based on performance indicators for 1998/99*; Arts Council of England; February 2000

[13] The analysis is based on the statistics provided for the Arts Council annual survey of regularly funded organisations for 1998/99

Graph 1: Dance organisations – spread of grants 1998/99

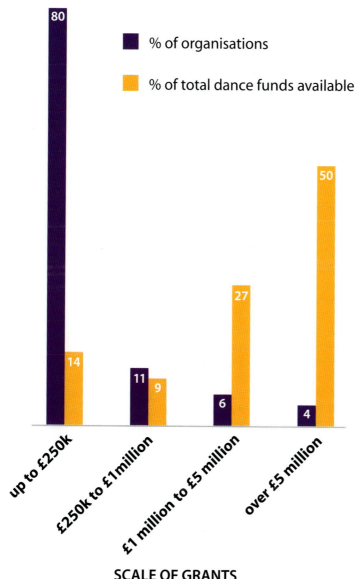

Regional spread

Graph 2 (overleaf) gives the number of organisations located in each region, and shows that most organisations are based in London.

Graph 2: Regularly funded dance organisations – regional spread, 1998/99

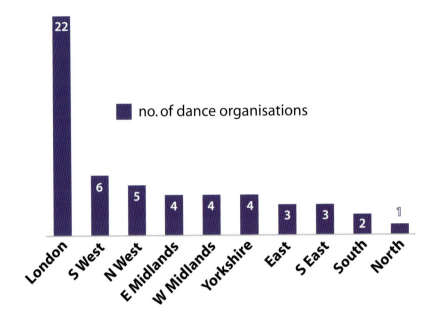

Graph 3: Regional spread of dance organisations and funds, 1998/99

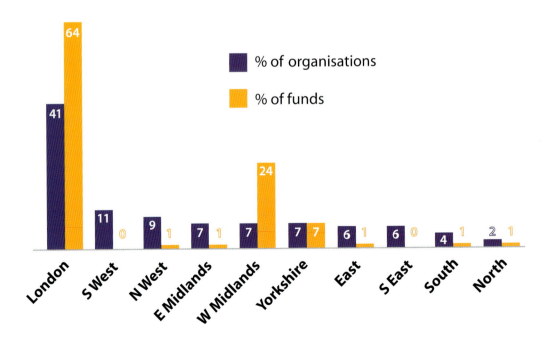

The purple columns in graph 3 show the percentage of all organisations based in each region.

The orange columns show the percentage of funds received by those organisations. This demonstrates that over 40% of organisations are based in London. This group includes most of the larger organisations and so receives almost 65% of the funds. The West Midlands looks relatively wealthy, but this is accounted for by Birmingham Royal Ballet, while Yorkshire Arts is the base for Northern Ballet Theatre.

Dance is still building its critical mass across the country and remains highly London-centric. Cities like Leeds and Birmingham, and areas such as the North West, and Swindon/Bath/Oxford, are developing a healthy mix of companies, spaces, venues, dancers, teachers and other artists. It will probably be at least another decade before dance communities are well established across the country. As with many artistic and cultural pursuits, London is the major production centre for dance and is likely to remain so for the foreseeable future.

Dance agencies

The regional spread of dance agencies is less London-dominated, as shown in graph 4 (overleaf). The purple columns show the percentage of all dance agencies by region. The orange columns show the percentage of all dance agency funds, also by region. London's high ratio of funds to number of organisations is accounted for by The Place, which incorporates the Richard Alston Dance Company, The Place Dance Theatre and The Place Dance Services. The South West's reverse position is accounted for by a network of county-based dance agencies and the lack of a National Dance Agency.

Graph 4: Dance agencies – regional spread, 1998/99

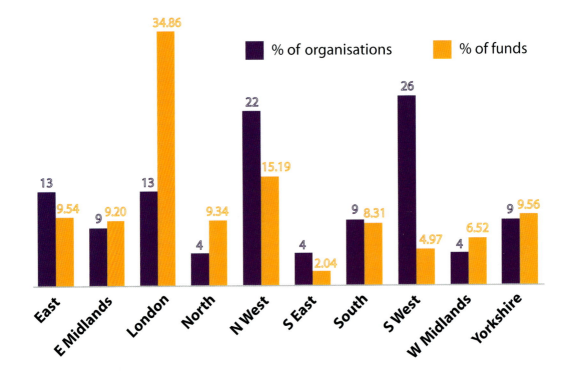

Types of dance

Companies work in different types of dance. Traditionally these are defined as ballet, contemporary, African, and South Asian. In addition, CandoCo and Salamanda Tandem integrate disabled and non-disabled dancers, and Green Candle and Ludus focus on work in education and community contexts.

Using all these definitions, graph 5 (right) summarises the diversity of provision. The first pie chart shows the distribution of regularly funded companies working in each type of dance. The second shows the number of new works created and the third, the number of performances. The fourth chart shows the size of audiences reached by each type of dance.

Graph 5: Types of dance – the diversity of provision, 1998/99

- ballet
- contemporary
- African
- South Asian
- dance & disability
- education

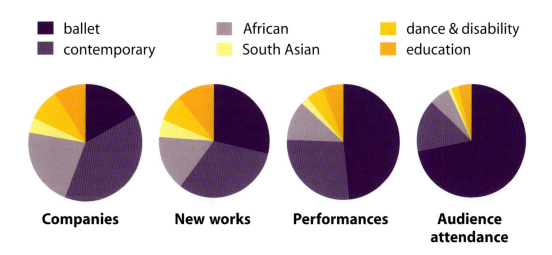

Companies **New works** **Performances** **Audience attendance**

Graph 6 (page 16) compares ballet companies with all dance companies, showing the number of companies, new works, performances, dancers' jobs and attendances.

The spending on ballet is high as a proportion of total expenditure on dance. However, it is comparable to large-scale work in, for example music, and provides value for money. In 1998/99 the leading ballet companies gave between 127 and 159 performances each, averaging 143 performances. Comparable opera companies gave between 103 and 129 performances each, averaging 116 performances. Subsidy per attendance for the ballet companies ranged from £9 to £41, while for the opera companies this ranged from £42 to £50. Ballet relies more on earned income, which represented between 21% and 45% of turnover; for opera, earned income represented between 19% and 22%. Opera is, however, more able to attract contributed income, which represented between 13% and 20% of turnover while for ballet the range was between 2% and 12%.

As highlighted in the Large Scale Touring Review (1998), venue and audience demand supports the amount of

RIGHT:
Birmingham Royal Ballet / Tombeaux

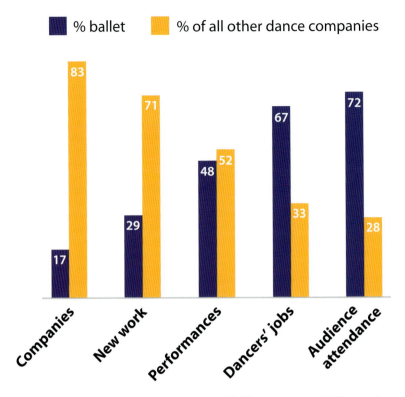

Graph 6: Ballet companies compared to all other dance companies, 1998/99

ballet available, and venues would like more middle-scale ballet and narrative-based dance. Structurally, this is the most stable part of the Arts Council funding programme and the one that provides the longest contracts and best working conditions for dancers. Reducing subsidy to ballet would result in less new work, less touring or increased seat prices – all of which go against Arts Council priorities. Despite the high proportion of Arts Council dance subsidy that ballet receives, the return on investment is high in terms of excellence, access and education.

Touring

National dance provision relies on the fact that all but one of the subsidised dance companies tour[14]. There are

14 The Royal Ballet no longer tours its Dance Bites programme, and only tours internationally

no dance companies with their own theatres. The Royal Ballet performs mainly at the Royal Opera House, which it shares with the Royal Opera, and Birmingham Royal Ballet is based in the Birmingham Hippodrome Theatre, which it shares with a range of art forms. Access to dance performances across the country is provided by touring companies. There are a number of key promoters who programme dance with energy and commitment, however a strong national network still needs to be consolidated. Too often dance companies expend a disproportionate amount of time, energy and resources in developing audiences for short runs. This is particularly onerous at the middle scale where management resources are leanest and touring dates are frequently for one or two nights.

Most dance touring is produced in London. For companies based in other parts of the country, the ability and funding to tour into London is important in terms of profile and artistic credibility, and has a direct impact on their ability to raise sponsorship. London also has a well-developed network of venues at different scales, namely Jackson's Lane, The Place, The Linbury Studio Theatre, the Purcell Rooms and Queen Elizabeth Hall at the South Bank Centre, Sadler's Wells and the Coliseum. They offer progression for artistic development, choice for audiences and a more rounded profile for dance than elsewhere in the country.

Large scale
On the large scale, touring tends to be by week. There is an established circuit co-ordinated by the National Dance Co-ordinating Committee and the Arts Council, which prevents clashes of companies and repertory. The 'sphere of influence' policy adopted following the Large Scale Touring Review, is working well and regular visits are developing audiences. For example, Northern Ballet Theatre finds the venues it visits twice a year are their best dates, suggesting that familiarity breeds audiences.

New, full-length, narrative work is provided by Northern Ballet Theatre, English National Ballet and Birmingham Royal Ballet and is winning both a loyal company following and audiences new to dance.

Middle scale
Contemporary dance tends to be created for the middle and small scale, but is frequently still perceived as 'high risk' by venue managers. Most bookings on these scales are for one or two nights, so touring costs are high. Audience development and marketing initiatives are cost and labour intensive, with limited opportunities for word-of-mouth and press coverage to impact on audience numbers. Frequently dance is booked only two or three times in a year, or as part of a dance week or at times when both little other product and limited audiences are available – such as bank holidays.

The middle scale remains crucial to the future of dance, in the short to medium term at least. There is greater diversity at this scale. Currently it includes Adzido, Shobana Jeyasingh, Richard Alston Dance Company, CandoCo, the Cholmondeleys and the Featherstonehaughs, DV8, and Siobhan Davies Dance Company. Provision at this scale is enhanced by companies such as Union Dance, Ricochet and Random Dance who are developing a presence on the middle scale. Between them, these companies provide a healthy mix of different cultural references including issue-based, abstract and narrative work; and dance with film, new music and sculpture.

Small scale
The small scale finds a log-jam of new and emerging dance artists, a mixture of future stars and work that has not yet found the imagination, production values or artistic power to win significant audiences. It provides the essential testing ground, but needs a better sifting system to really contribute to audience development. Imaginative

Adzido Pan African Dance Ensemble / Sankofa-Dance: Adzogbo from Benign

promoters can make it work, for example Swindon Dance's Taking Risks seasons and the Woking Dance Umbrella Festival, but it requires work, creativity and investment. Part of the problem is the significance the arts funding system has traditionally placed on touring and audiences. With few other funding rationales available, too many companies are chasing too few dates with work that is of variable quality.

Promoter choice

The number of British touring dance companies beyond the regularly funded ones reaches 90[15], not including a fluid group of touring projects. In addition, a number of venues regularly promote international dance. For example in 2000/01, international work accounts for 66% of Sadler's Wells dance programme, with a similar amount programmed for 2001/02. The Peacock Theatre regularly programmes flamenco and other international work, while The Place and the South Bank integrate international work into their regular programmes. Festivals such as Dance Umbrella, Nott Dance, Brighton and Edinburgh play a key role in bringing in international work, and companies such as the Trockaderos and Nederlands Dans Theatre are becoming regular features on the touring dance landscape.

International exchange is important to artistic development, and international touring contributes to the profile and self-esteem of dance artists. Promoting British dance overseas requires them to be more competitive when compared to highly subsidised native companies elsewhere. Greater effort needs to be put into international advocacy through networking, and attending conferences and seminars.

Promoters have a wide artistic choice, and their choice is more sophisticated than dance form alone. For

15 Taking together all the companies listed in *A Booker's Guide to British Dance* and the British Council's *British Dance in profile 2000*, including graduate companies, and companies based in Scotland and Wales. See appendix 4.

example, within African and South Asian dance there are companies taking traditional and contemporary approaches. There is Irish, jazz, street dance, carnival, aerial work, and East Asian dance. While most small and middle-scale companies are working in western contemporary dance, this includes artists concerned with narrative, abstract form, issues and different techniques in various combinations.

Small-scale contemporary dance includes a number of regularly funded companies, and a very large number of project funded ones. Additional funding support for dance is received through regional arts boards and the Touring Department of the Arts Council. However, the demand for funding from this sector far outstrips the funding system's ability to respond. In 1998/99 the Arts Council received 66 applications for project funding, amounting to £1,435,280. It was able to respond to less than half – 31 awards amounting to £716,525, an average grant of just over £23,000. This sector includes vital emerging companies, long-established artists and companies working regularly but dependent on project funding. Access to larger funds such as the Regional Arts Lottery Projects (RALP) and the National Touring Programme (NTP) should, over time, benefit this sector. This is beginning to happen already – for example, between November 1999 and November 2000, the NTP spent about £1.2million on a total of 34 dance projects, giving an average grant of over £35,000.

Venues
Dance is still building a strong national network of venues suited to dance. A large proportion of venues were built as playhouses for the presentation of drama. Dance companies need to continue to develop ever-closer relationships with venues. A growing number of promoters appreciate and want to book dance, and they put significant time and effort into their dance programming, but financial restrictions frequently

frustrate their ambitions. While some venues commission dance occasionally, the notion of the dance producer is rare. Until the funding announcement of March 2001 theatres had been facing their own crisis, with shrinking resources resulting in the need to maximise income and reduce costs. This is hardly a fertile situation for innovative, contemporary and challenging artistic product. Different ways of disseminating dance are emerging that could reduce the reliance on traditional touring practice, find new audiences and new ways of engaging with audiences[16].

The debates highlighted in the Boyden Report[17] and the Arts Council's response in *The Next Stage*[18] have more potential for dance but have still to be explored. Helpful models are emerging, such as the consortia of larger venues working together to promote a tour of Adventures in Motion Pictures' production of Car Man and exploring the possibilities of commissioning work. Dundee Rep is home to Scottish Dance Theatre, but there is no equivalent model in England. The Arts Council's framework for an emerging National Policy for Theatre in England provides an opportunity to encourage closer relationships between companies and venues, especially on the larger scales.

Beyond theatres

Beyond the theatre context, dance is having a powerful impact with work produced for less traditional sites. Examples include Genesis Canyon at the Natural History Museum, and dance created for bridges, motorways, rail stations, sports centres and outdoor spaces around the country. In August 2000, the Akademi's Coming of Age project featured 100 professional and student dancers of all ages performing a range of South Asian dance styles to audiences of some 10,000 in and outside London's South Bank Centre. Such events are, in every sense,

[16] Dance Meet, 8 June 2000

[17] *Roles and Functions of the English Regional Producing Theatres*; Peter Boyden Associates for the Arts Council of England; May 2000

[18] *The Next Stage*; Arts Council; May 2000

RIGHT:
Dance Umbrella / Genesis Canyon

extraordinary. They take excellent art to people, create spectacular theatre and transform our everyday lives and experience of our environment.

Overview

Artistically, the under-resourced independent sector is driving creativity and pushing the art form forwards, while the bulk of public subsidy is directed at a small number of large companies. Examples of sharing resources are emerging, and are valuable and healthy. They also highlight the poverty gap in the quality of working spaces and conditions. Artistic collaborations are hampered by differing working practices[19] and inequality in resources between collaborators. A critical shortage of male dancers has followed years of under-investment in dance in schools and vocational training provision. Recently, a production had to be cancelled when calls to 20 male dancers found that none were available for work[20].

Further warning signals appeared during the course of this study. Particular and different issues facing organisations including Birmingham Royal Ballet, CandoCo, Dance UK, English National Ballet, Green Candle Dance Company, Northern Ballet Theatre, Siobhan Davies Dance Company and Union Dance underlined the need to resource capacity for change. Too frequently key issues such as planning for succession, organisational development, contingency planning, creative reinvigoration and risk-management are simply not an option for dance organisations. Too many of England's key individuals and companies in dance are living an itinerant, hand-to-mouth existence that belies their true significance. The relentless drive to respond to crisis is cheating audiences and suppressing excellence, and it is taking its toll on artists and managers across dance.

19 For example, commissions crossing boundaries between artistic and cultural forms need quality preparation time to enable dancers to learn new movement languages

20 The production was a revival by Dansconnect scheduled for The Place in May 2000

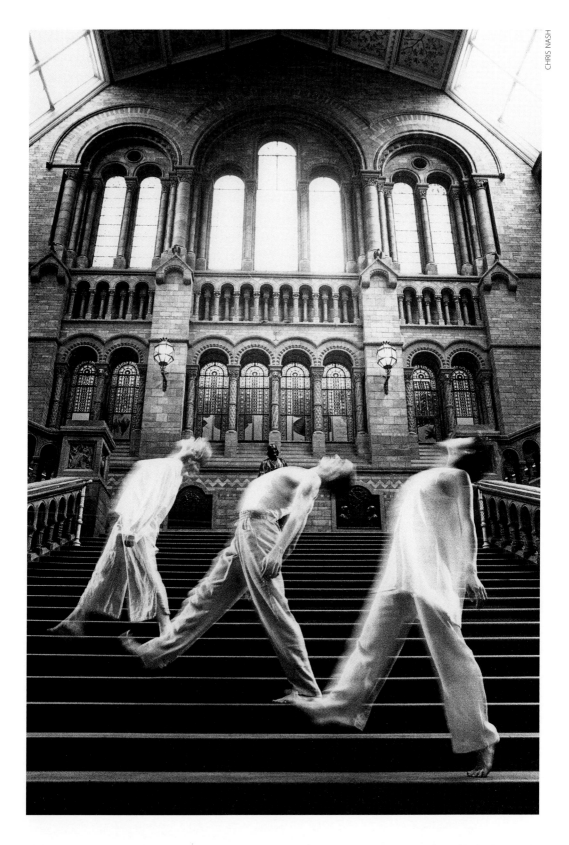

Looking back over dance development in the 1990s, it's clear that the arts funding system played a critical role in nurturing an emerging art form to the point of maturity. The seeds of a national dance infrastructure are in place. Diverse artistic languages have been encouraged, together with methods of production more suited to the nature of dance creation and dissemination. Artists nurtured through public subsidy have developed commercial enterprises and dance is reaching more parts of the country and more of the population than before. Influence has been exercised to secure a foothold for dance in the national curriculum and limit the worst extremes of the threat to vocational training provision. Some skirmishes have been won, but there are more battles to be fought. Not everything has been achieved to the level hoped for; this is essentially a factor of operating in a dynamic environment in which artistic resources have outstripped financial ones.

3
Situational analysis

THE ART

There is a lack of balance in dance provision that needs to be addressed if the art form is to be sustained, nurtured and developed. On the large scale, the dance that reaches the largest audiences is predominantly balletic. New work is being created, but there is little evidence of new developments in the language of ballet, either in this country or internationally, of the order of those forged by Balanchine or Forsythe. The traditional definitions of ballet and contemporary are becoming blurred as new work draws on a range of traditions, vocabularies and techniques. Audiences and artists continue to want large-scale dance, and are perhaps less concerned with definitions than with the vision and the quality of the dance experience.

Creative energy is evident on the smaller scale, but too many emerging artists set up companies and seek to tour work at too early a stage. More opportunities for young creators to experiment, collaborate with more experienced artists, and to park work for subsequent development would encourage artistic growth and diversity. Dancers need to dance, and need to perform in order to develop their artistry. Bigger casts and longer rehearsal periods would provide jobs for dancers and enhanced spectacle for audiences. More, imaginative partnerships between promoters, agencies and artists would provide opportunities for dancers, research and development environments for choreographers, encourage risk and innovation, and build relationships with audiences – but not necessarily all at the same time and within the same project.

The Arts Council is committed to supporting artists, enabling them to follow their creative instincts, take risks and experiment[21]. This need was highlighted in the Independent Dance Review Report[22] and recognised by the introduction of Dance Fellowships in 2000/01. This is a good example of the kind of flexibility that the arts funding system needs in order to address artists as individuals.

The art form is interrogating and debating its structures, practices and assumptions; and looking to its own resources to make a difference. There are signs of a shift towards greater cohesion and coherence across the sector, shown through an increased willingness to network, share resources and expertise, and to tackle issues collectively. Examples include the Association of National Dance Agencies working together to mount the British Dance Edition festival in 2002; Northern Ballet Theatre and Phoenix Dance sharing teachers, providing a joint summer school and planning a shared new building in Leeds; and the Artists Development Initiative run by the Royal Opera House that makes their dance studios and managerial expertise available to selected independent artists[23]. Dance is eager to build partnerships across and beyond the profession. It is hungry to invent and experiment, and push at the boundaries of real and virtual presentation, the contexts and purposes of participation, and the meanings and applications of art in society.

Essentially collaborative, dance provides work, creative opportunities, exposure and audiences for artists in a wide range of disciplines. Choreographers collaborate regularly with composers and musicians, and increasingly

[21] Support for the Individual Artist, current Arts Council policy

[22] *Independent Dance Review Report*, Gill Clarke and Rachel Gibson; June 1998

[23] Other examples include the Dance Open meeting, January 2000, and Dance UK's Healthier Dancer Programme

with other artists, for example sculptors. Dance provides a particularly important platform for new music, and dance productions incorporate stage, lighting and costume design.

The process of creating and presenting dance is about people working together. Choreographers are creating and refining new languages and accents, catching the essence of the moment and affecting people's lives, perceptions and understandings. Increasingly the role of the dancer is as a vital contributor to the creative process. Dancers are reaching higher standards of technical excellence, physicality and performance power, and moving between the roles of creator, performer, educator, advocate and promoter with more speed and facility. Dance managers are increasingly being entrepreneurial, finding new contexts, relationships and ways of making best use of human and financial resources[24]. This way of working brings its own stresses and anxieties. Most dance professionals are young, reflecting the rapid growth of activity, but increasingly the sector will need to be able to support senior professionals. Funding and support systems need to be people-focused, aim to protect against burn-out and promote the possibility of lifelong careers in dance.

Education and participation in dance have a strong tradition. Changes in the funding of 'animateurs' have transformed many into 'dance development officers', resulting in a subtle but profound change in emphasis. There is a need to identify and profile the best practice, debate and promote continual development. Conferences such as 'The Edge of Creativity', organised by the Foundation for Community Dance, can make a big difference in ensuring that dance remains at the cutting edge across a wide range of social, educational, regenerative and civic contexts.

Liz Lehrman, Artistic Director of Liz Lehrman Dance

[24] For example, Siobhan Davies Dance Company made a management training film using dance as a metaphor for change and creativity in business contexts. Other examples would include site-specific work and participatory projects

Exchange, talks of needing to 'hike the hierarchies'[25] from vertical to horizontal, to create a continuum that extends across all kinds of dance and all forms of engagement in dance. There are many hierarchies to be hiked and hegemonies to be broken. Breaking the hegemony of traditional models of touring would allow for greater innovation and relevance in reaching audiences. Breaking the arts funding system's reliance on audience numbers as indicators of value for money would validate a broader range of practice. Recognising participation, education, community dance, site-specific work, dance on film and TV, digital dance and so on as effective and valid means of engaging people with dance would open up more access routes and make dance more inclusive.

The quality of work has to be the first consideration. Audience expectations are continually rising, particularly regarding the standards of dance and the production values. Strengths in youth, community and education work cannot be allowed to turn to complacency. Dance practitioners must be enabled to keep pushing at boundaries and keep honing the cutting edge in all forms of practice and engagement.

ECONOMICS

Producing dance is an expensive undertaking. A high proportion of work is devised in the studio with the dancers; the processes of creation and production are symbiotic. Dance production costs include music, design and the hire of space managed by other arts organisations. So, the production of dance is an economic driver that benefits the wider arts sector. Public subsidy to dance needs to be seen in this wider artistic and economic context.

The processes of creation, production, marketing and touring dance are out of synchrony. Too often the

[25] Catalytic Conversions, 25 May 2000

V-Tol Dance Company / Where Angels Fear to Tread

product has to be sold and marketed before it has been created. While the market might welcome revivals, artists tend to want to create new work and the logistics of mounting a revival can be even more complex for companies that work on a project basis and do not have a permanent, full-time company of dancers. This is true of all but six dance companies.

Around 240 dancers' jobs are with the four ballet companies, which represent about two-thirds of all dancers' jobs. Only a further 44 jobs offer annual contracts[26]. The rest offer short-term contracts ranging from 10 months to a few weeks. Dancers need to sustain

[26] Figures taken from the British Council's *British Dance in profile 2000*

a maintenance regime that includes regular class both during and between periods of work. Access to affordable, high quality professional class is essential to sustain employability especially for the growing population of freelance dancers who work on a project basis with a range of companies. About a third of all dancer jobs bring limited access to regular class, physiotherapy and other injury prevention programmes, and work that takes place in rented spaces of variable suitability. This is the area of greatest mobility of independent dancers, whose number is far greater than the number of jobs normally available. They are at greatest risk of injury and have least support to prevent and manage it.

Dancers' careers are short and precarious. Many will embark on their careers with debt accumulated over three or four years of full-time training. Given the paucity of other work, for example adverts or sessional work, they need improved salaries while in work in order to ensure their future employability both as a dancer and once dancing is no longer an option. The need for improved salaries, better salary scales and working conditions are critical factors for the longer-term health of dance. The alternative will be a continued drain of expertise and experience out of dance, which in the longer-term wastes valuable investment and resources, and inhibits development. Opportunities for continuous professional development for dancers, teachers, choreographers, managers and all dance practitioners are needed to encourage the flow of expertise and the emergence of leaders.

Improved salaries, working conditions and opportunities for career progression are needed to build the capacity and the confidence of those working across dance. The dance community itself needs to raise its sights, celebrate its achievements and be more ambitious. It needs to raise its expectations of its practice, to ensure continually

CandoCo Dance Company / Sunbyrne

improving quality and innovation, and to expect realistic fees, terms and conditions, and profile in return. Developing new partnerships across and beyond the cultural sector would extend the reach of dance. Building stronger partnerships with local authorities, venues and business that go beyond the narrow confines of sponsorship or bookings has the potential to create a more robust economic base for the sector. Achieving this also requires confidence.

With relatively few sustainable commercial outlets for dance, demand for public investment is, understandably, greater than the funds available. The financial fragility of the sector makes the inevitable competition especially painful, and makes it critical that the core group of dance artists and organisations is adequately funded. Building capacity within organisations is needed to facilitate planning for success and succession.

ACCESS

The elements are in place. Dance is in touch with young people and multicultural Britain. Dance agencies, touring companies and the cultural diversity of dance are all vital strengths in need of adequate support. There are routes to facilitate access to careers in dance, but the profile of students in full-time vocational training is predominantly white, middle-class and female.

Cultural and demographic diversity in dance needs to better reflect the nature of society as a whole. This means addressing under-representation, for example of men and those from a range of cultures as dancers. Additionally, we need more women and people from a wider range of cultures working as artistic directors and senior managers within the large-scale companies. Profile, access, education, networks, training, role models, advocacy and positive action can all play a part in achieving this objective. Significant numbers of children dance but, until recently, few dance productions have been created specifically for younger audiences. As the sector matures, an increasing number of older dancers want to continue performing. The last few years have seen a number of experiments in this area[27], and this trend might be expected to continue.

Dance is achieving much, but too quietly. It has not yet reached the critical mass or profile that will ensure it is always on the agenda beyond the arts community. Public perception and understanding about dance needs to be raised, broadened and brought up to date. Its significant contribution to areas such as health, education and social regeneration, as much as to excellent and innovatory art, are all stories waiting to be told. Bold artistic statements, risk and challenge will engage people in talking about artistic issues and make dance relevant to their everyday lives. The work needs to be exciting and provocative, and needs to be brought to public attention.

27 For example, Anne Dickie's project *From Here to Maturity*, supported by London Arts

4
Mapping the future

IMPORTANT TRENDS

The future cannot be mapped, but neither can it be ignored. Unless we face the future we are in danger of proposing solutions for yesterday's problems. It is possible to predict various trends on the basis of what we know today, and wise to explore their implications for the future for dance.

The age profile of tomorrow's population will be different. By 2010 there will be 2 million fewer 25–34 year olds and nearly 3 million more 45–64 year olds, and a significant increase in over 75 year olds[28]. This is 'not simply an extension of old age, but an extension of every phase of the life-cycle'[29]. We will be younger and older for longer; we will acquire more experiences, make more choices and experience more different lifestyles in a single lifetime than our predecessors. Predicting the expectations and behaviour of artists and audiences on the basis of their age will become increasingly unreliable[30]. The population will be increasingly diverse and individual.

The trend towards a cash-rich/time-poor population will continue. We will have more disposable income but less

[28] *Towards 2010: new times, new challenges for the arts*, The Arts Council, 2000

[29] Gerard Lemos, Catalytic Conversions, 27 April 2000

[30] *The Age Shift*, Ageing Population Panel, Foresight, 1999

time, and face growing competition for both. Technological developments build redundancy into an increasing range of products and there is a growing choice of options for spending leisure time. A quarter of the population is already online, and the last 10 years has seen an increase in magazines, radio and TV channels. There are more means of receiving information and communicating with other people than ever. Life is getting faster and more connected. We will increasingly build communities around shared interests as much as around geographical location. Increasing choice will raise expectations and further contribute to real and perceived exclusion for a growing range of groups in society. Price will continue to be a factor, but 'value' will be a subtler, more pervasive driver and will be assessed by a wider range of criteria.

People will increasingly look for value for time, not just for money. We will have more media but shorter attention spans. The generations brought up with digital media will be more visually literate, have greater facility with scanning large quantities of data and with handling fast cuts and edits. We will be more demanding audiences, wanting special experiences and high impact art in short bursts. We will be less generous about seeing potential in emerging or second-rate work. At the same time, we will retain many of the core values we adopt in our formative years throughout our longer lives. Transience, metaphor and allegory will become special and sought after qualities, contrasting in quality with the speed and soundbites of the everyday, and allowing the time, space and magic squeezed out by demanding lifestyles.

INTERACTIVE CONSUMPTION

We will be more demanding in other ways. DVD already offers us choice of viewing angle. Will we continue to be as accepting of the artist's right to select our viewpoint?

Digital interactivity offers even more choice, and increasingly it will be possible to deliver dance to computer screens in our homes and workplaces. Will this trend lead us to interact with online choreography, to play art alongside intergalactic battles and fantasy football? Pay-to-view TV is bringing new meanings to our understanding of a commodity. Will we come to expect to pay for art experiences, as long as they are at times and in places and formats that we choose? The demarcation between production and consumption is shifting. 'We are increasingly implicated in producing what we consume… Consumption is becoming more interactive and often the last stage of the production process'[31]. The audience is necessarily implicated in its own experience of art. To an extent this has been a cause of unease with art at times when our expectation of consumption has been mainly materialistic. New expectations of consumption and new notions about commodities are potentially conducive to new kinds, roles and purposes of art.

IMPLICATIONS FOR DANCE

The digital age

It might be assumed that the traditional theatrical experience will have reducing appeal on the basis of these trends, but audiences are still increasing for dance[32]. This might reflect something about the nature of dance being in tune with the moment, with a growing interest in the transient and allegorical, and in balancing the physical, intellectual and emotional aspects of being human. Antony Gormley, sculptor, said recently that his 'passion for dance comes from a strong conviction that it is the most direct form of communication possible between beings. It is about physical empathy'[33].

Dance's various associations with glamour, theatricality,

31 Charles Leadbeater; *Living on Thin Air*; Penguin, 1999

32 TGI and Premier TGI findings, 1999

33 Antony Gormley, Catalytic Conversions, 27 April 2000

Cholmondeleys and Featherstonehaughs / Car

communal experience, collaboration with a range of art forms, and site-specific performance already provide the special events that transport us beyond the ordinary and everyday. With its evident strengths in recreational, community and educational contexts, dance delivers 'live' interactive arts experience. With no language barrier, it is a powerful cultural ambassador. Digital media is content-hungry, and digital dissemination recognises no geographic boundaries. Audience-driven websites such as www.ballet.co.uk and www.criticaldance.com are offering new opportunities for dance enthusiasts to create communities of interest on an international scale. Online debates are democratising the traditional role of the critic, and blurring the boundaries between artist, audience and pundit.

Future-facing paradigms highlight a number of paradoxes. Digital media has the potential to create dance commodities, forge new markets and reduce funding dependency. Increased commercialism and funding independence could bring more subtle changes, enhancing confidence and assurance as a result of wider endorsement. Such welcome shifts are predicated on a medium that is highly susceptible to piracy, and require a commercial acumen that is rarely nurtured by a public funding paradigm with its emphasis on public service. Encouraging risk, flexibility and entrepreneurship requires the possibility of significant gain and a basic level of security. Yet core funding has hardly provided either in recent years. Aspirations for greater cultural diversity have to take note of a decade of decline in funding for vocational training, resulting in access to a career in dance being limited by finance, geography and public policy. Ambitions for innovation, challenge and strong individuals are at variance with the processes of training, working practices and funding that encourage conformity rather than difference and back institutions rather than individuals.

Backing potential

Traditional assumptions have to be questioned, and new routes found through the paradoxes to realise the potential of dance and ensure that audiences and participants have access to the widest range of highest quality dance. We need to identify, nurture and back the people who will carry dance forwards, whether or not they are currently working in traditional roles and organisations.

We need to recognise too that the world beyond dance works on words. While kinaesthetic images are powerful and pervasive, dance needs to be as articulate with words as it is through movement. Writing about dance has made academic advances, but reviews remain scarce and issue-based features even rarer. Few dance personalities feature as interesting media commentators, even on arts issues. To an extent this reflects the nature of dance, an apologetic culture and a still-developing critical mass. Stronger dialogue, debate, opinion, passion, conflict and 'spin', would engage the general public, vitalise the language of dance, raise its profile and open new access routes.

There are opportunities to be seized, both in the wider cultural and demographic landscape and in the strengths of dance. In order to respond to such opportunities an integrated approach is needed. It must address the fundamental fragility of the infrastructure and also empower individuals to drive the future-proofing of dance. We cannot predict the next creative spring. We cannot know where, when or how it will become manifest, but it will happen and is likely to be driven by an individual. Too often the arts funding system has been caught on the back foot, tied into strategies focused on short-term outputs, rather than long-term outcomes. It is time to choreograph a step-change, to get on the front foot and build in the capacity to be future-ready, if not future-proof.

5
Priorities for investing in 21st century dance

The vision for investing in 21st century dance weaves together strengthened core support and shifts in approach, which are focused on individuals, companies, looking to the future and creating the climate in which dance can thrive.

INVESTING IN INDIVIDUALS

The **dance artists fellowship programme** should be continued and developed into a rolling programme, open to dancers as well as choreographers. The programme offers time for artistic growth, artist-driven working practices and most significantly it is investing in tomorrow's creative and interpretative artists. The pilot programme, operating in 2000–02, supports seven artists and has been welcomed by the sector. The programme focuses on developing the artist's individual voice, strengthening confidence and prompting bold, risky steps forward.

Encouraging **dance entrepreneurs** through a programme complementary to the dance artists fellowship

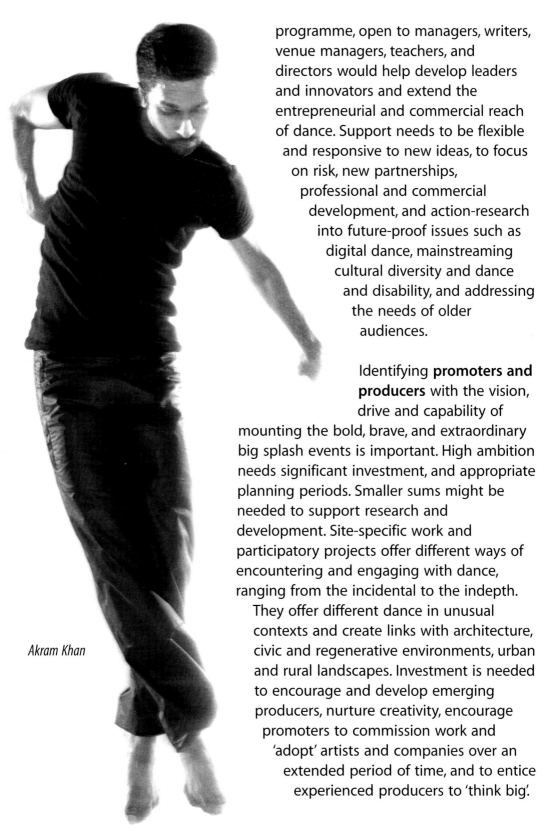

Akram Khan

programme, open to managers, writers, venue managers, teachers, and directors would help develop leaders and innovators and extend the entrepreneurial and commercial reach of dance. Support needs to be flexible and responsive to new ideas, to focus on risk, new partnerships, professional and commercial development, and action-research into future-proof issues such as digital dance, mainstreaming cultural diversity and dance and disability, and addressing the needs of older audiences.

Identifying **promoters and producers** with the vision, drive and capability of mounting the bold, brave, and extraordinary big splash events is important. High ambition needs significant investment, and appropriate planning periods. Smaller sums might be needed to support research and development. Site-specific work and participatory projects offer different ways of encountering and engaging with dance, ranging from the incidental to the indepth. They offer different dance in unusual contexts and create links with architecture, civic and regenerative environments, urban and rural landscapes. Investment is needed to encourage and develop emerging producers, nurture creativity, encourage promoters to commission work and 'adopt' artists and companies over an extended period of time, and to entice experienced producers to 'think big'.

STRENGTHENING COMPANIES

Large-scale companies need adequate core funding to maintain the classical ballet tradition, the growing contemporary heritage, and nurture new voices. Additional support might be directed at new work, increased touring weeks, education projects and improved working conditions and career development for dancers.

Middle and larger small-scale companies are in crisis, and funds are needed urgently to save several from closure. Beyond this, enhanced production values and bigger casts will better meet audience and venue expectation, while different and more appropriate creation and dissemination practices will better support artistic achievement. Increased management capacity is critical and needs to include better salaries and the possibility of continuing professional development and improved status for managers working at this scale. Training, career development, marketing, international networking and entrepreneurial skills are needed to ensure dance business managers are equipped to complement the creative energy of artistic directors.

Greater diversity needs to be encouraged among **small and emerging companies**. This might include new relationships with venues, and new ways of working and engaging with audiences, for example digitally, through platforms, debate, and participatory projects. Talent must be backed, but not forced into a relentless cycle of making and touring work. Funds need to respond to artists' self-determination and encourage them to enter the arts market with new, diverse and individual approaches to dance creation and dissemination.

Random Dance Company / The Trilogy

FACING THE FUTURE

Seismic shifts in attitudes, cultures and practice are most effectively forged through influence, relationships and funding initiatives. Examples might include:

- promoting partnerships with advertising agencies
- positioning dance more strongly in the health sector
- developing the commercial acumen to exploit the commodification of dance
- contributing to advocacy for a more vibrant arts and creativity curriculum

Such initiatives require ensuring best practice, quality and new knowledge within dance, as well as a more alert watch beyond dance to help it reach its full potential role in society.

Facing the future means being prepared for the unexpected, having the capacity to respond to the next creative springs and the **blue skies**. This might be an individual artist with an unprecedented vision, a sudden flurry of promoters with big ideas, or a sudden upsurge in audience demand. Creative energy continually outstrips investment; if there continues to be no means of responding then the springs of creativity will become clogged with disenchantment and despondency.

Dance is strong in the field of **new technology and media**. It is well placed to deliver sought-after interactive arts experiences. There is a need for further investment in these areas to build on past successes such as Digital Dancing and Dance for Camera, and to help dance extend its reach in terms of presentation, dissemination and audience development through broadcast/narrowcast and other technological opportunities.

CREATING THE CLIMATE

Cultural diversity needs special attention. Mainstream education, the vocational training infrastructure and creation and dissemination processes, are all based on western dance models. The issues relating to the still-developing critical mass for dance are even sharper for culturally diverse dance. Work has to be better supported, with enhanced management and marketing, and brought into the arts infrastructure at all levels. Opportunities for creative experiment, networking, mentoring and debate are also needed.

Strategic organisations, including the Dancers Trust, Dance UK and Foundation for Community Dance require adequate core funding to respond rapidly to issues and opportunities, as part of an ongoing partnership with artists to forge seismic shifts. Their research, profile, advocacy and services benefit the whole of dance by building capacity, confidence and visibility.

Dance agencies are laying the foundations for the development of dance communities, providing education and community programmes, recreational activities, affordable space for dance creation and participation, and increased local profile. Enhanced core funding would build on a decade of small but effective investment. It would enable increased education activity, associate artists programmes with management support, mentoring and critical feedback. Professional development, stronger local partnerships, new producers and different ways of engaging with local audiences are also needed. The potential for extending the network of National Dance Agencies to reflect the significance of, for example, Derby Dance Centre and Greenwich Dance Agency, should also be examined.

Regional developments must nurture regional dance cultures. Increased resources at regional level would promote local involvement, and facilitate healthy dance communities with a sustainable mix of artists, spaces, venues, audiences and companies. Metropolitan areas are likely to be the most fertile, and this can be seen in, for example, London, Leeds, the North West and Birmingham. Groupings of towns, for example Swindon/Oxford/Bath/Bristol, and Derby/Nottingham demonstrate the advantages of encouraging growth that reflects opportunities for dance and the existence of transport systems. Rural areas have different opportunities and needs. A renewed focus on the regions and a strengthened role for local authorities in nurturing their local dance ecologies should promote enhanced civic pride in dance.

THE RESULTS

Shifts in emphasis need to be made to build the capacity for dance to be future-ready, if not future-proof. Relatively modest sums are needed to avert disaster – dance has not been in a position to accumulate large deficits. The strategic deployment of funds has the potential to take dance from survival to success.

In return, dance has the potential to increase the quality, diversity and number of performances, to engage a broader range of people in meaningful dance experiences and play its full role in society as a whole.

It is time to face the future. The opportunity to leap confidently forward is here. It requires investment, ambition and risk. In return, dance can guarantee creative diversity, challenge, innovation and the potential to provide socially relevant, dynamic and inspiring experiences for the artists and audiences of the 21st century.

APPENDIX 1

A short history of dance
(with special reference to Arts Council of England funding)

1945 Sadler's Wells Theatre Ballet reopens the Royal Opera House after WWII with Sleeping Beauty, and takes up residence. Ballet Rambert and Ballets Jooss are the only other dance companies supported by the Arts Council.

1950s Martha Graham brings her company to London for the first time. Beginnings of wider interest in new, contemporary dance languages.

1960s Rambert becomes a modern ensemble company. London School of Contemporary Dance and Company founded. Beginnings of British contemporary dance.

1970s London Contemporary Dance Theatre undertakes residency tours, first three animateurs appointed (Swindon, Cheshire, Cardiff), taking contemporary dance to local communities with an emphasis on access, education and participation. X6 and the emergence of the independent dance artist. Arts Council Music Department employs a ballet and dance officer. London Arts Board employs a dance and mime officer.

1979 Arts Council establishes its Dance Department.

1980s Number of animateurs grows to over 80, with seed funding from the Arts Council. Establishment of National Association of Dance and Mime Animateurs (NADMA, now the Foundation for Community Dance) following ACE conference. First Dance Umbrella Festival.

Establishment of National Organisation for Dance and Mime (now Dance UK). Increase in number of companies, eg Extemporary Dance Theatre, Mantis, Janet Smith and Dancers. Culturally diverse dance forms become more visible. Growth of dance in education companies including Ludus, and development of education programmes by larger dance companies. Growth of youth dance. First dance degrees (Laban Centre) dance in higher education (Surrey, Middlesex). Regional arts boards (RABs) employ dance officers.

1989 *Stepping Forward: some suggestions for the development of dance in England during the 1990s*, by Graham Devlin, commissioned for the Arts Council Dance Department.

1990s Establishment of National Dance Agencies, many growing from animateur projects, eg Swindon Dance. Emergence of choreographer-led dance companies, eg the Cholmondeleys, Adventures in Motion Pictures. Increase in the number of companies and independent artists. Increased awareness of issues related to status of dance, spaces, working conditions, Healthier Dancer Programme, training and support for administrators. Dance established in the national curriculum. Growing interest in site-specific work, and dance in special settings such as prisons, hospitals.

2000 Devolution of NDAs and development funds to RABs. The Arts Council introduces Fellowships for individual artists.

APPENDIX 2

Growth in Arts Council funds for dance
1969/70 to 1998/99

	1969/70 £	1979/80 £	1989/90 £	1998/99 £
Grant in aid (Arts Council of Great Britain/Arts Council of England)	8,200,000	63,125,000	155,500,000	189,950,000
At 1969/70 prices	8,200,000	19,414,134	23,482,505	20,289,319
Arts Council expenditure on arts in England	6,456,000	48,613,000	147,428,000	188,293,000
Total expenditure on dance (Note: 1969/70 and 1979/80 includes opera)	1,587,892	8,718,290	12,244,467	23,236,478
At 1969/70 prices	1,587,892	2,681,316	1,849,072	2,481,981
Dance as percentage of expenditure on arts in England	25%	18%	8%	12%
Expenditure on dance, excluding Royal Opera House, Royal Ballet, Birmingham Royal Ballet	187,892	1,718,290	4,666,967	11,364,198
At 1969/70 prices	187,892	528,461	704,772	1,213,855
As percentage of expenditure on arts in England	3%	4%	3%	6%
Number of organisations supported	7	31	64	74
Average grant at 1969/70 prices	26,842	17,047	11,012	16,403

APPENDIX 3

Regularly funded dance organisations in England 1998/99

Organisation	Location	Funding body	Regular Arts Council/RAB funding 1998/99
Adzido Pan African Dance Ensemble	London	ACE	680,016
Badejo Arts	London	ACE	95,940
Birmingham Royal Ballet	WMidlands	ACE	5,417,280
Bristol and Bath Dance Consortium	South West	SWA	10,500
CandoCo Dance Co	London	ACE	90,000
Cheshire Dance Workshop	North West	NWAB	38,000
Chisenhale Dance Space	London	LA	92,000
Cholmondeleys & F'haughs	London	ACE	182,000
Dance 4	EMidlands	ACE	125,000
Dance Agency Cornwall	South West	SWA	11,500
Dance City	Northern	ACE / NAB	169,000
Dance Initiative Greater Manchester	North West	NWAB	20,000
Dance Northwest	North West	ACE / NWAB	60,000
Dance Services	South West	SWA	30,000
Dance UK	London	ACE	85,000
Dance Umbrella	London	ACE	268,000
DanceXchange	WMidlands	ACE / WMAB	118,000
Derby Dance Development	EMidlands	EMAB	41,500
Dorset Dance Forum	South West	SWA	8,000
DV8 Physical Theatre	London	ACE	165,000
East London Dance	London	LA	22,000
English National Ballet	London	ACE	3,871,776
Essexdance	Eastern	EAB	20,000
Foundation for Community Dance	EMidlands	ACE	75,000
Gloucester Dance Project	South West	SWA	10,000
Green Candle Dance Co	London	ACE	130,000

Organisation	Location	Funding body	Regular Arts Council/RAB funding 1998/99
Hampshire Dance Trust	Southern	SAB	12,500
IRIE! Dance Theatre	London	LA	38,000
Jabadao	Yorkshire	YA	38,000
Kadam Asian Dance and Music	Eastern	EAB	6,000
Kokuma Dance Theatre	WMidlands	WMAB	233,300
Ludus Dance Agency	North West	NWAB	132,000
Merseyside Dance Initiative	North West	NWAB	25,000
Motionhouse Dance Theatre	WMidlands	WMAB	98,200
Northern Ballet Theatre	Yorkshire	ACE	1,215,200
Phoenix Dance Co	Yorkshire	YA	312,250
Rambert	London	ACE	1,278,000
Richard Alston Dance Co	London	ACE	420,000
Royal Ballet	London	ACE	6,455,000
Sadler's Wells Theatre Trust	London	LA	220,000
Salamanda Tandem	EMidlands	EMAB	20,945
Salongo	South West	SWA	20,000
Shobana Jeyasingh Dance Co	London	ACE	210,000
Siobhan Davies Dance Co	London	ACE	306,000
South East Dance Agency	South East	SEAB	37,000
Suffolk Dance	Eastern	ACE / EAB	146,600
Swindon Dance	Southern	ACE / SAB	138,000
The Place	London	ACE / LA	517,000
Union Dance Company	London	ACE / LA	97,200
University of Surrey	South East	SEAB	10,000
V-Tol Dance Co	London	ACE	103,000
Woking Dance Umbrella	South East	SEAB	45,000
Yolande Snaith Theatredance	London	ACE	75,000
Yorkshire Dance	Yorkshire	ACE / YA	135,000
TOTALS	54		24,179,707

ACE = Arts Council of England
EAB = Eastern Arts Board
EMAB = East Midlands Arts Board
LA = London Arts
NAB = Northern Arts Board
NWAB = North West Arts Board
SAB = Southern Arts Board
SEAB = South East Arts Board
SWA = South West Arts
WMAB = West Midlands Arts Board
YA = Yorkshire Arts

APPENDIX 4

Touring dance companies
as listed in *A Booker's Guide to British Dance* and the British Council's *British Dance in profile 2000*

4D Dance Co	Claire Russ Ensemble
Aletta Collins Dance Co	Clerkinworks
Adventures in Motion Pictures	The Curve Foundation
Adzido Pan African Dance Ensemble	Dansconnect
Air Dance Co	David Massingham Dance
Akram Khan	Divas
Arc Dance Co	Diversions Dance Co
Attic Dance Co	DV8 Physical Theatre
BABE – Bad-Ass Ballerinas Ensemble	earthfall
Badejo Arts	English National Ballet
Bedlam Dance Co	Fight or Flight
Bi Ma Dance Co	Flying Gorillas
Birmingham Royal Ballet	Green Candle
Bock & Vincenzi	H Patten
Laurie Booth and Company	Images of Dance
British Gas Ballet Central	INTOTO Dance
Carol Brown Dances	The Jazz Dance Company
Mark Bruce Dance Co	IRIE! Dance Theatre
A Buckley/P Hampson	Javier de Frutos
Bullies Ballerinas	Jazz Art UK
Carlson Dance Co	JazzXchange Music & Dance
CandoCo Dance Co	Jiving Lindy Hoppers
Charles Linehan	Jeremy James Co
The Charnock Company	Jonathan Burrows Group
Cholmondeleys & Featherstonehaughs	Kokuma Performing Arts

Kultyer Dance Theatre	Rosemary Butcher Dance Co
Rosemary Lee	Royal Ballet
Ludus Dance Co	Russell Maliphant Dance Co
The Mark Baldwin Dance Co	Sakoba Dance Theatre
Matthew Hawkins Company	Sankalpam
Michael Clark Company	Scottish Ballet
Mixed Doubles	Scottish Dance Theatre
Momentary Fusion	Sean Tuan John
Motionhouse Dance Theatre	Shobana Jeyasingh Dance Co
Nahid Siddiqui and Company	Siobhan Davies Dance Co
National Youth Dance Company	Srishti
Northern Ballet Theatre	Small Bones Dance Co
Phoenix Dance Company	Transitions Dance Co
Physical Recall	Union Dance
Rambert	Vincent Dance Theatre
Random Dance Co	V-Tol Dance Co
Retina Dance Co	Walker Dance
Richard Alston Dance Co	Wendy Houston
Ricochet Dance Co	Yolande Snaith Theatredance
RJC	The X Factor Dance Co

APPENDIX 5

Sources

This study began by reviewing the findings of recent intra-sectoral reports, namely:
- Review of South Asian Dance in England (July 1997) *
- Review of large-scale touring (April 1998)
- Independent dance sector review report (June 1988) *
- Time for change: a framework for the development of African People's dance forms (August 1999) *

It also draws on:
- Arts Council Annual Reports *
- Statistical survey of regularly funded organisations 1998/99 *
- Notes of the Catalytic Conversions series of seminars (available at www.artscouncil.org.uk/futurealert/)
- Towards 2010: new times, new challenges for the arts, 2000 *
- The Age Shift, Ageing Population Panel, Foresight, 1999
- Target group index results reports, Peter Verwey, Arts Council of England
- Roles and Functions of the English Regional Producing Theatres, report by Peter Boyden Associates for the Arts Council, May 2000 *
- The Next Stage, Arts Council, May 2000 *
- The Creativity Imperative, New Statesman Arts Lecture 2000 *
- Discussion papers on support for the individual artist, continuing professional development
- Stepping Forward: some suggestions for the development of dance in England during the 1990s, by Graham Devlin *
- A Booker's Guide to British Dance, Dance UK
- British Dance in profile 2000, the British Council
- Ballet, an illustrated history, Mary Clarke and Clement Crisp, Adam and Charles Black, London, 1974

It has been informed by various discussions with key players including the Arts Council Advisory Panel for Dance; Arts Council Dance and Touring Department; Panel Working Group: Christopher Bannerman, Stephen Barry, Rachel Gibson, Jane Mooney; National Dance Co-ordinating Committee, Management Liaison Group and Dance Meet 2000.

*These publications are all available from the Arts Council of England.

Index

Access 3, 34, 39

Audiences 9, 18, 19, 27, 30, 34, 35, 38

Cultural diversity 6, 19, 34, 45

Dance
  companies: 3
    large scale 15, 18, 27, 43
    middle scale 16, 19, 43
    small scale 19, 22, 27, 43
  education:
    in the community 3, 9, 29, 30, 44
    in schools 14, 24, 44
  forms:
    African 14
    ballet 3, 14, 15, 16, 27
    contemporary 14, 27
    dance and disability 14, 42
    digital 37, 39, 42
    new media 45
    South Asian 6, 14, 23
  organisations: 10, 45
    Dance UK 3, 6, 45, 50
    Dancers Trust 45
    Foundation for Community Dance 3, 6, 9, 29, 45, 49
    National Dance Agencies 3, 4, 13, 28, 46, 50
  venues/sites: 18, 21, 22
    site-specific 23, 38, 42

Development organisations 5

Funding 10–16, 51
  fixed-term 5
  grants 10, 22
  investment 6, 41
  National Touring Programmes (NTP) 22

Regional Arts Lottery Projects (RALP) 22
regularly funded organisations 4, 22, 52
system 3, 26, 40

Individual artists 41
    animateurs 3, 29, 49
    artistic directors 34, 42
    choreographers 29, 41
    dancers:
        continuous professional development 31, 41
        health and safety 32
        salaries 32

International work 21

Management 43
    producers 23, 42
    promoters 21, 22, 42, 45

Regions 46
    RABs 4, 10, 50

Reports/research
    Boyden 10, 23
    Devlin 1, 50
    Independent Dance Review 6, 28
    Large Scale Touring Review, 1998 15, 18
    National Mapping Research Project, 2000 9

Social inclusion 26

Touring 16, 18, 19, 21, 54